Creative Light Wood Carving

J. MATTHEWS

Metricated Edition

EDWARD ARNOLD

© J. MATTHEWS 1975

First published 1968
by Edward Arnold (Publishers) Ltd.,
25 Hill Street, London W1X 8LL

Reprinted 1969, 1972
Metricated Edition 1975

ISBN: 0 7131 1939 X

By the same author:

Pictorial Woodwork

    BOOK ONE   – Background to Wood; Construction; Finishes
    BOOK TWO   – Tools and Their Correct Use
    BOOK THREE – A Guide to Practical Work

Further Creative Light Wood Carving

The Stanley Book of Sculpture with Surform Tools

(from Rank Audio-Visual Ltd)

Six filmstrips entitled: The Creative Light Wood Carving Series

Printed by offset in Great Britain by
William Clowes & Sons, Limited, London, Beccles and Colchester

Preface

The approach to free line shaping and carving developed through this book stimulates the pupil's interest immediately and leads to considerable enthusiasm and skill in creative work.

The book is suitable for most ability ranges in Secondary schools and is particularly valuable for the average and the slow pupil. There is an unlimited selection of subjects to carve, from ancient weapons and animals to cars and rockets, and the method and tools illustrated do not require the fuller technique of true wood carving.

According to the teacher's discretion the book can be used as an interesting introduction to woodwork for first-year pupils or as a pleasant change from formal construction.

The book comprises four main sections which progress from two- to three-dimensional work: 1. *Wall Carvings*: The pupil is introduced to simple edge and face shaping on one side only and to the innumerable possibilities of free line design; 2. *Standing Carvings*: This project takes the pupil on from single- to double-face shaping; 3. *Bowl Carvings*: Pupils learn to incorporate functional design into their work, involving gouging technique; 4. *Abstract Sculpture*: The pupil is free to produce a carving entirely from his imagination or individual observation and to employ the knowledge gained of the correct use of tools and shaping processes.

Each section is introduced by photographs of groups of carvings and a general introduction. Where necessary, there follows a full-size outline and a photograph of one or two practice pieces with working guides to help pupils obtain the necessary basic shaping experience while working together as a class. With the shaping experience gained and using the design guide in each section pupils should be able to work individually on original projects. The book ends with a general guide to the pupil for producing an abstract wood sculpture of his own creation.

I wish to express my thanks to my wife Marian; and to Speare & Jackson Ltd, Aetna Works; C. & J. Hampton Ltd, Record Tool Works; Wm. Marples & Sons

Ltd, Hibernia Works; Stanley Works, Ltd; Storman Archer Ltd, Fitzwilliam Works; Ware & Payne Ltd, Limbrick Works; all of Sheffield, who gave considerable help in compiling this book.   Also to E. C. Young, Homerton Bridge, London, Timber Merchants; Fitchett & Woollacott Ltd, Nottingham; and my special thanks to the photographers, Maltby & Griffiths Ltd, Kirkby-in-Ashfield, Nottinghamshire.

The work photographed in the book was made by pupils at Westbourne County Secondary School, Sutton-in-Ashfield, Nottinghamshire.

A practical note

When choosing timber for carving the ideal method is to arrange the paper patterns on suitable boarding so that the grain is used to the best advantage. This should be thoroughly supervised so that it does not lead to unnecessary waste.

If at first each pupil's carving area is not converted to a workable overall marking-out size, difficulties may arise in coping-sawing and fixing in the vice. The method by which the timber is brought to the overall size, whether by circular saw or rip saw, etc., is thought best left to the discretion of the teacher.

It is very important that the correct method of using a coping saw is demonstrated thoroughly and a constant watch kept for incorrect sawing technique. The wood rasp and wood file are often illustrated for edge shaping, etc. These tools will produce good results if they are applied to cut with the forward stroke only, whereas edge shaping, etc., with a spokeshave is often very difficult on end grain or for working small and abrupt curves.

In two sections of the book guidance for initial bulk tapering with a jack plane is illustrated. This reduces the bulk waste easily, and forms a guide for working a supple shape.

Sometimes it is very difficult to cut in eyes or a mouth, and often the carving looks better without them.

Contents

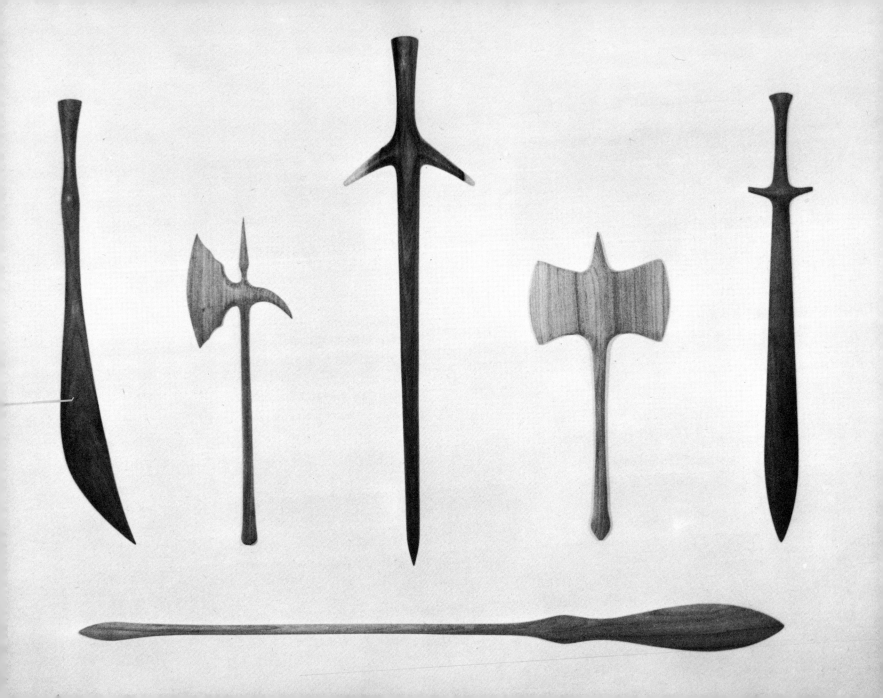

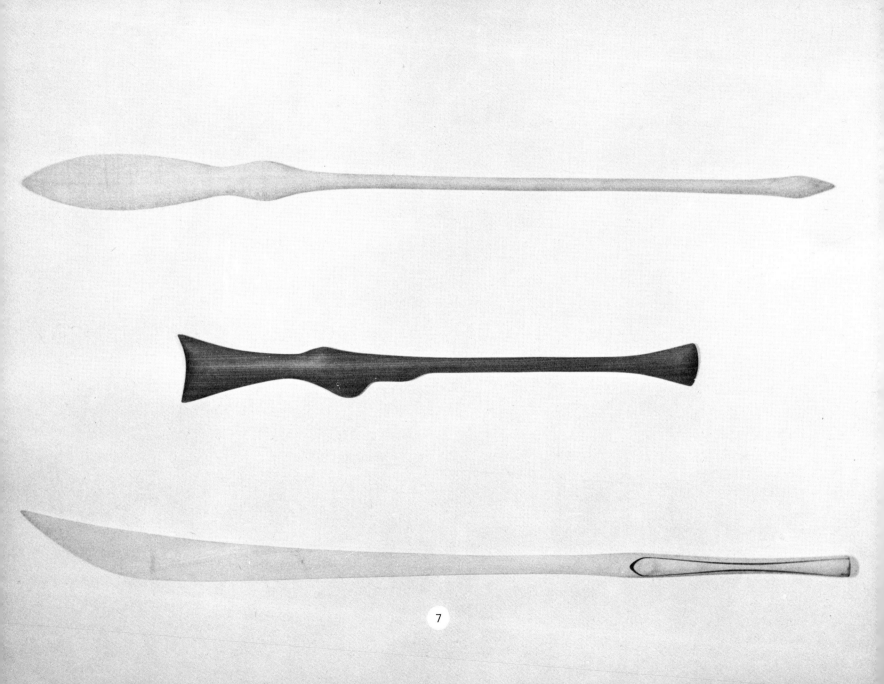

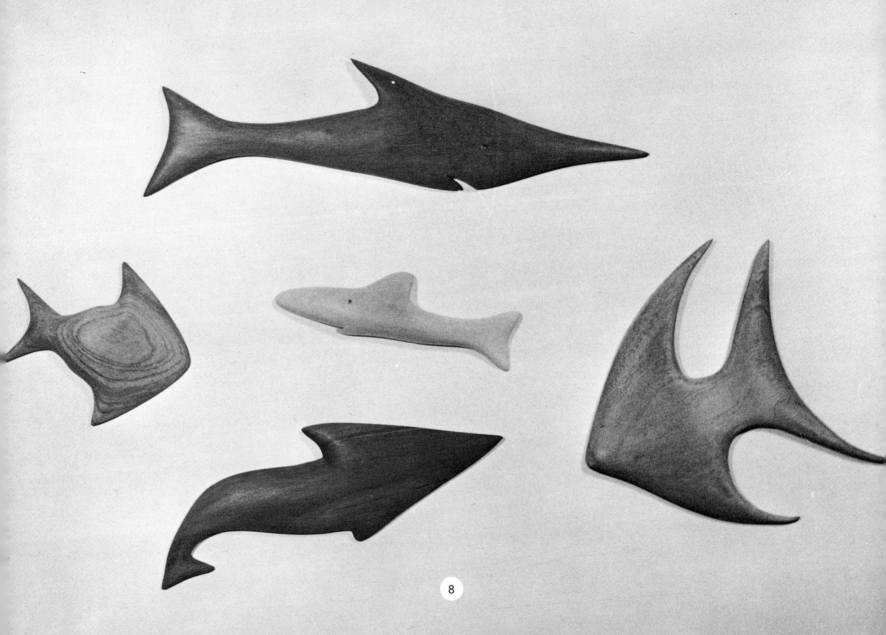

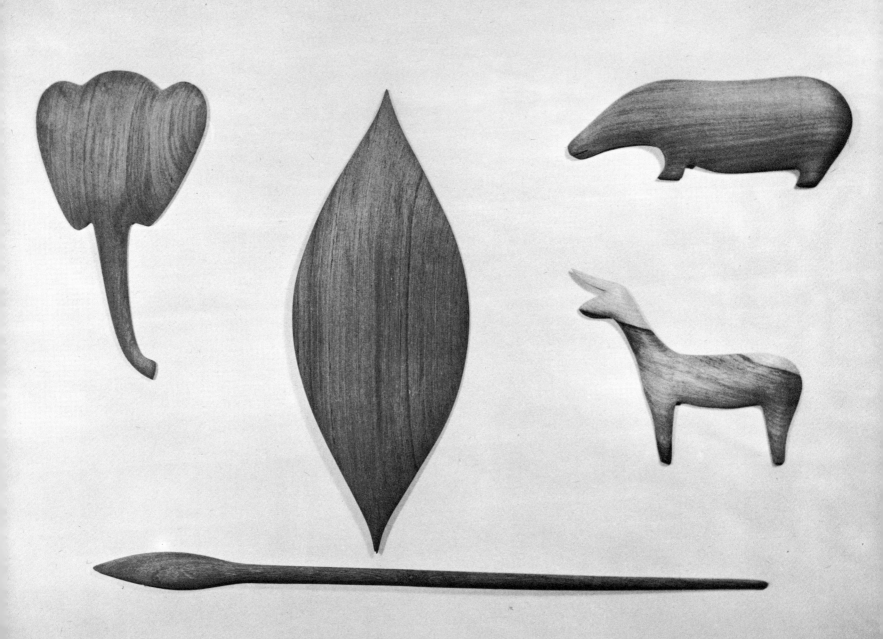

INTRODUCTION TO WALL CARVINGS

❶

A WALL CARVING CAN BE AN ATTRACTIVE FITMENT
ON THE WALL OF YOUR HOME

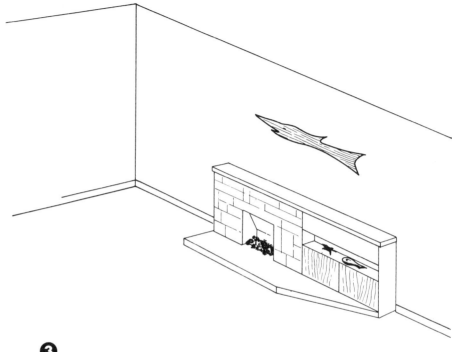

❷

THE FRONT OF A WALL CARVING IS ROUNDED

❸

THE BACK IS FLAT TO FIT FLUSH TO THE WALL

11

❹

THE CARVING CAN BE FASTENED TO THE WALL WITH CONTACT ADHESIVE

INTRODUCTION TO WALL CARVINGS

❺

USE A CLEAN CUTTING HARDWOOD FOR EASY WORKING

E X A M P L E S

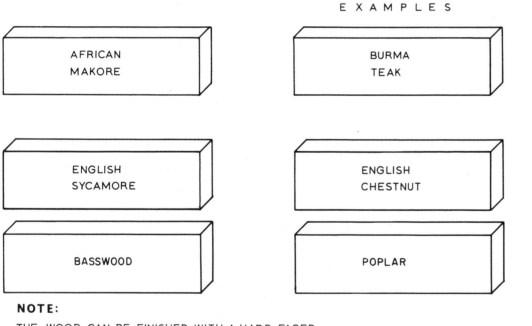

AFRICAN
MAKORE

BURMA
TEAK

AFRICAN
MANSONIA

ENGLISH
SYCAMORE

ENGLISH
CHESTNUT

ENGLISH
WALNUT

BASSWOOD

POPLAR

MAHOGANY

NOTE:

THE WOOD CAN BE FINISHED WITH A HARD FACED
LACQUER OR OIL- OR IT CAN BE LEFT IN ITS NATURAL STATE.
CHOOSE THE FINISH TO SUIT THE TYPE OF TIMBER

❻

TO GAIN EXPERIENCE MAKE
ONE OF THE SET PIECES BY
FOLLOWING THE WORKING GUIDE

WORKING GUIDE FOR WALL CARVING SET PIECE Nº1

MAKE A TRACING OF THE
FULL SIZE OUTLINE BELOW

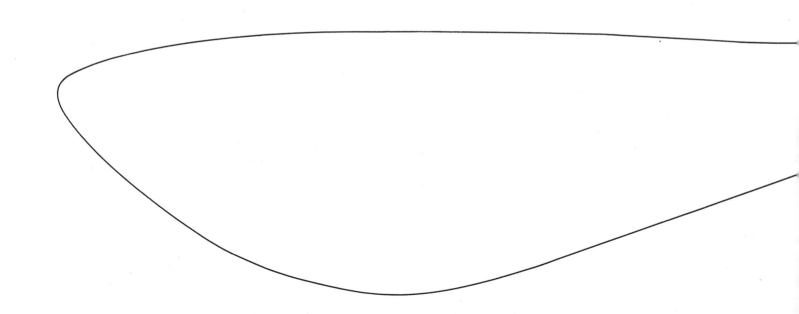

WORKING GUIDE FOR WALL CARVING SET PIECE Nº 1

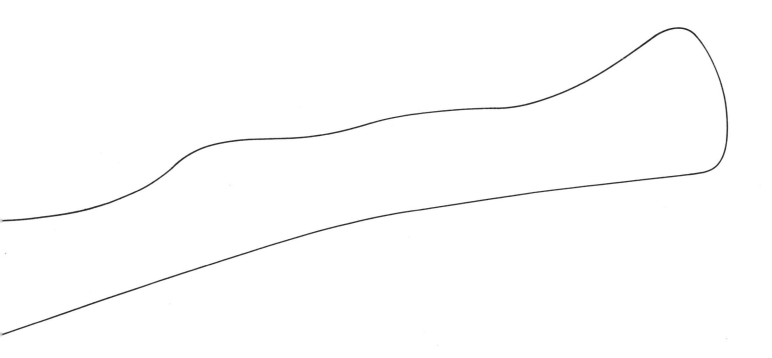

WORKING GUIDE FOR WALL CARVING SET PIECE No 1

2

FROM A SUITABLE LENGTH OF MACHINE
FACE-PLANED AND THICKNESSED NATURAL
BOARDING PREPARE A PIECE OF TIMBER
TO THE OVERALL MARKING OUT SIZES BELOW

1' 6" (458 mm)

5/8" OR 3/4"
(16 mm
OR 18 mm)

3½"
(90 mm)

3

MARK OUT THE BLADE'S TAPER WASTE

6"
(152 mm)

5/16"
(8 mm)

COLOUR IN THE WASTE

WORKING GUIDE FOR WALL CARVING SET PIECE № 1

4

REMOVE THE WASTE WITH A JACK PLANE
(LEAVE THE LINES JUST IN)

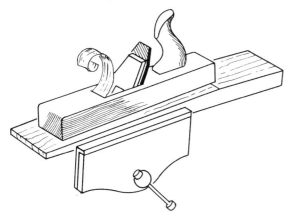

5

PIN YOUR TRACING ON THE BACK OF YOUR
TAPERED TIMBER AND TRACE OVER WITH A 3H PENCIL

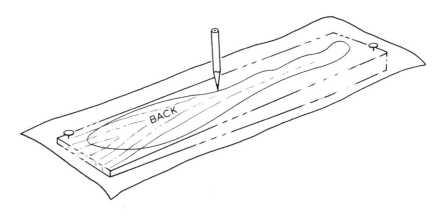

BACK

6

REMOVE THE TRACING PAPER AND
PENCIL IN THE PENCIL IMPRINT

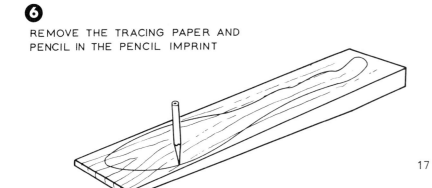

7

COLOUR IN
THE WASTE

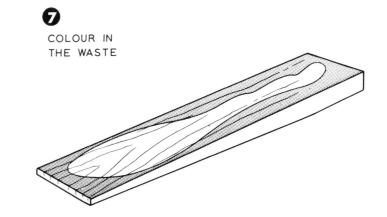

8

AT A SUITABLE POSITION
MARK OVER A SQUARE
SAWING GUIDE LINE

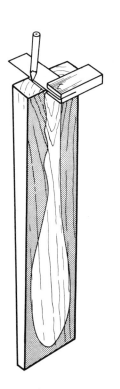

9

REMOVE THE WASTE
WITH A COPING SAW
(LEAVE THE LINES WELL IN)

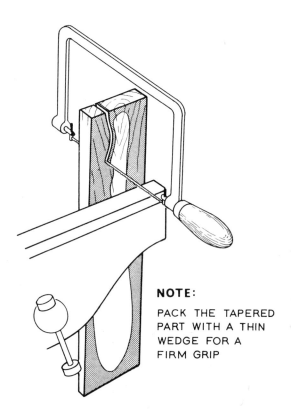

NOTE:

PACK THE TAPERED
PART WITH A THIN
WEDGE FOR A
FIRM GRIP

18

WORKING GUIDE FOR WALL CARVING SET PIECE №1

10

REMOVE ANY LARGE LUMPS LEFT
BY THE SAW DIAGONALLY WITH
A MEDIUM CUTTING WOOD RASP

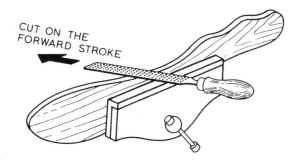

CUT ON THE
FORWARD STROKE

11

FINISH OFF WITH A FINE
CUTTING CABINET FILE
(LEAVE THE LINES JUST IN)

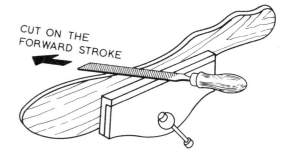

CUT ON THE
FORWARD STROKE

12

FINGER GAUGE ⅛" (3 mm)
LINE FROM THE BACK
ALL ROUND THE EDGE

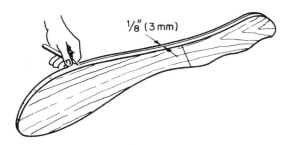

⅛" (3 mm)

13

MARK A LINE DOWN THE
CENTRE OF THE HANDLE
TO THE POINT OF THE BLADE

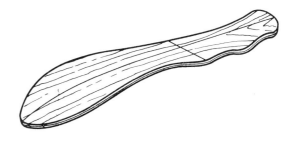

WORKING GUIDE FOR WALL CARVING SET PIECE № 1

14

COLOUR IN THE WASTE

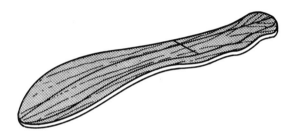

15

ROUND OFF THE WASTE USING A SPOKESHAVE
A MEDIUM CUTTING RASP AND FINE CUTTING
WOOD FILES
(LEAVE THE LINES JUST IN)

SUPPORT

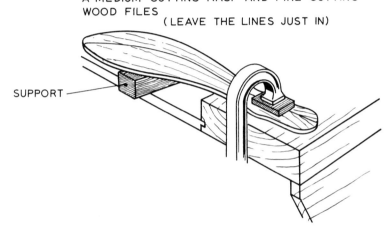

16

CLEAN UP WITH GLASS PAPER
GRADE №M2 THEN GRADE №1
OR SANDPAPER GRADE №80 THEN
GRADE №120

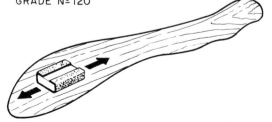

17

APPLY

A

FINISH

?

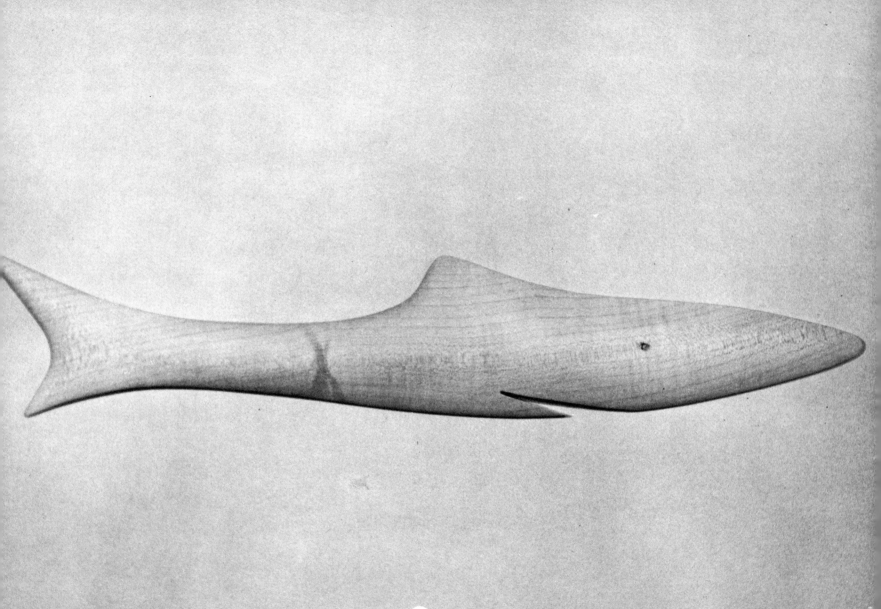

WORKING GUIDE FOR WALL CARVING SET PIECE Nº2

MAKE A TRACING OF THE
FULL SIZE OUTLINE BELOW

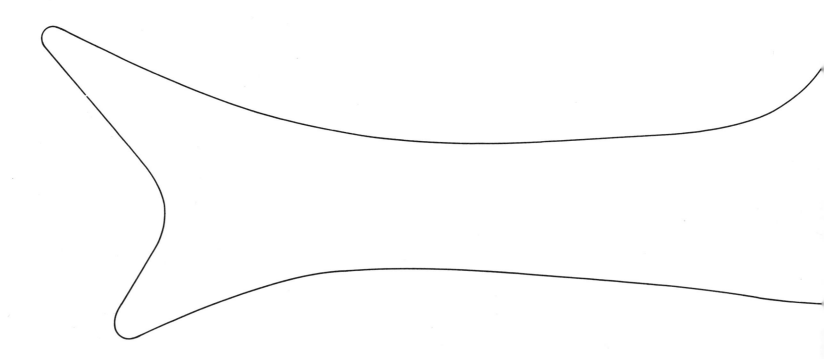

WORKING GUIDE FOR WALL CARVING SET PIECE №2

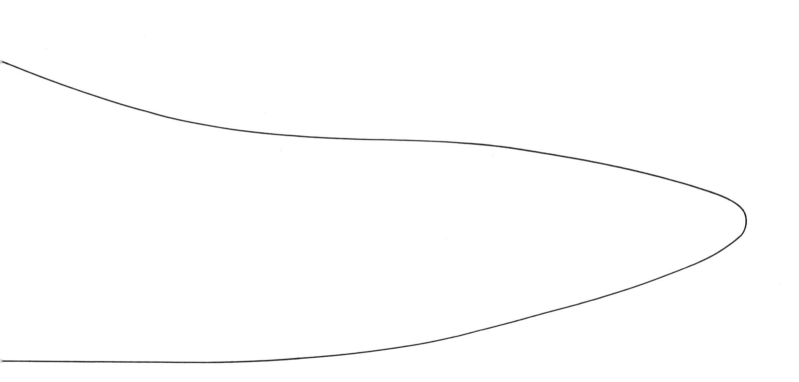

WORKING GUIDE FOR WALL CARVING SET PIECE Nº2

2

FROM A SUITABLE LENGTH OF MACHINE
FACE PLANED AND THICKNESSED NATURAL
BOARDING PREPARE A PIECE OF TIMBER
TO THE OVERALL MARKING OUT SIZES BELOW

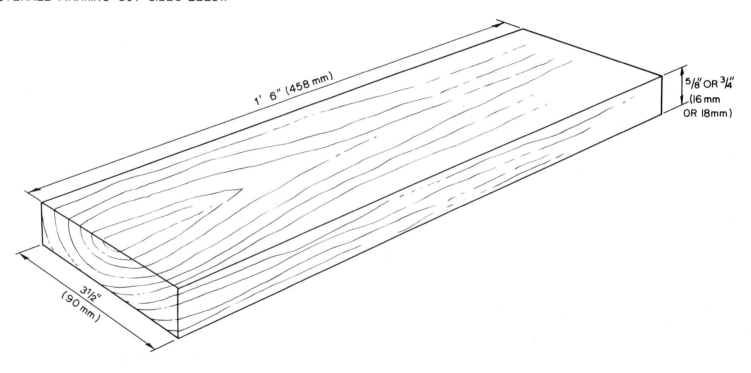

1' 6" (458 mm)

5/8" OR 3/4"
(16 mm
OR 18mm)

3½"
(90 mm)

WORKING GUIDE FOR WALL CARVING SET PIECE Nº2

❸

MARK OUT THE NOSE TAPER
AND THE TAIL TAPER
         (GUIDE BELOW)

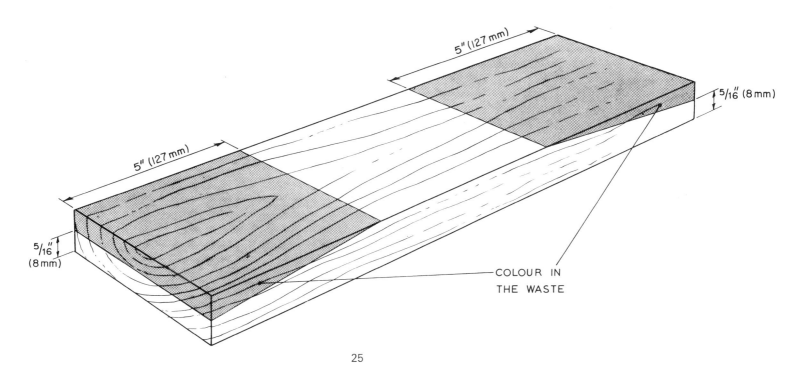

5" (127 mm)

5" (127 mm)

$\frac{5}{16}''$ (8 mm)

$\frac{5}{16}''$ (8mm)

COLOUR IN
THE WASTE

WORKING GUIDE FOR WALL CARVING SET PIECE Nº2

4

REMOVE THE WASTE
WITH A JACK PLANE
(LEAVE THE LINES JUST IN)

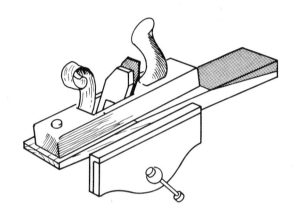
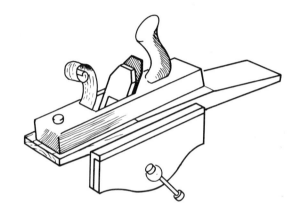

5

PIN YOUR TRACING ON THE BACK OF THE TAPERED
TIMBER AND TRACE OVER WITH A 3H PENCIL

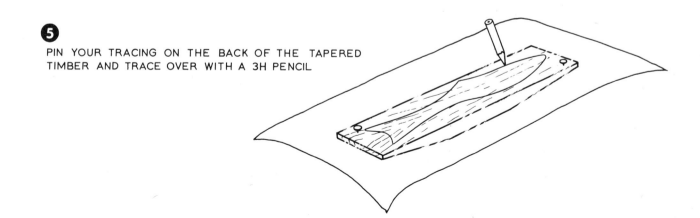

WORKING GUIDE FOR WALL CARVING SET PIECE Nº2

6 REMOVE THE TRACING PAPER
AND PENCIL IN THE IMPRINT

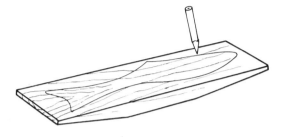

7 COLOUR IN
THE WASTE

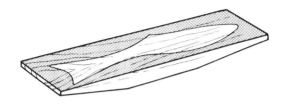

8 AT A SUITABLE POSITION
MARK OVER A SQUARE
SAWING GUIDE LINE

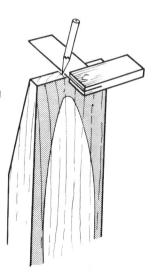

9 REMOVE THE WASTE
WITH A COPING SAW
(LEAVE THE LINES JUST IN)

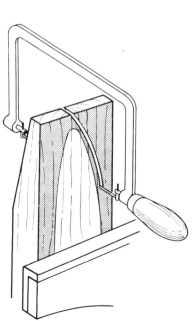

WORKING GUIDE FOR WALL CARVING SET PIECE Nº2

⑩

REMOVE ANY LARGE LUMPS LEFT
BY THE SAW DIAGONALLY WITH
A MEDIUM CUTTING WOOD RASP

⑪

FINISH OFF WITH A FINE
CUTTING CABINET FILE

(LEAVE THE LINES JUST IN)

CUT WITH
FORWARD STROKE ONLY

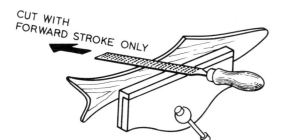

CUT WITH
FORWARD STROKE ONLY

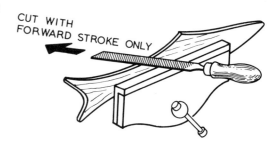

⑫

FINGER GAUGE 1/8" (3 mm)
LINE FROM THE BACK
ALL ROUND THE EDGE

⑬

BEND A THIN LATH FROM THE CENTRE
OF THE NOSE TO THE CENTRE OF THE
TAIL AND MARK ON A CENTRE LINE

1/8" (3 mm)

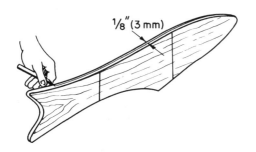

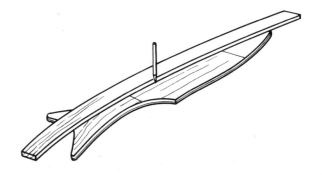

WORKING GUIDE FOR WALL CARVING SET PIECE №2

14

COLOUR IN THE WASTE

15

ROUND OFF THE WASTE USING A
SPOKESHAVE, MEDIUM CUTTING RASP,
AND A FINE CUTTING WOOD FILE
(LEAVE THE LINES JUST IN)

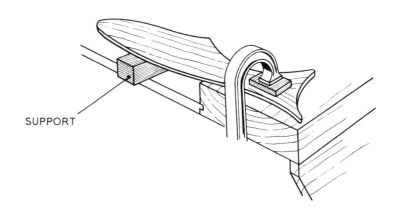

SUPPORT

16

WORKED RESULT

WORKING GUIDE FOR WALL CARVING SET PIECE Nº2

 17

MARK OUT THE MOUTH, COLOUR IN THE WASTE, AND SAW IT OUT CAREFULLY

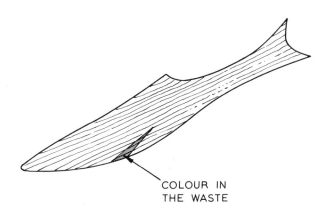

COLOUR IN
THE WASTE

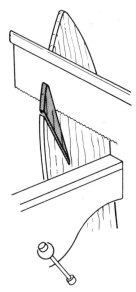

 18

MARK THE EYE POSITION AND
BORE OUT WITH A BRADAWL

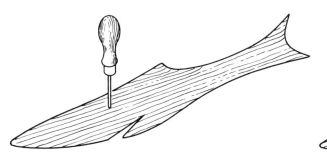

 19

CLEAN UP WITH GLASS PAPER
GRADE Nº M2 THEN GRADE Nº 1
OR SANDPAPER GRADE Nº 80 THEN
GRADE Nº 120

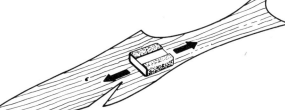

 20

APPLY

A

FINISH

?

A GUIDE FOR DESIGNING A WALL CARVING

❶

FIRST DO A NUMBER OF REASONABLY SIZED SKETCHES
ON THICK PAPER OF SUITABLE THINGS TO CARVE

❷

IDEAS FOR SKETCHES CAN BE OBTAINED

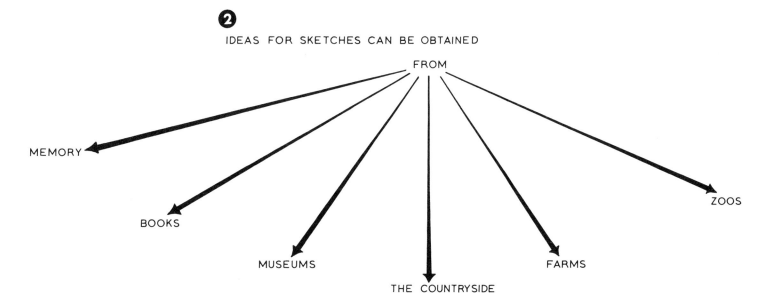

FROM

MEMORY

BOOKS

MUSEUMS

THE COUNTRYSIDE

FARMS

ZOOS

A GUIDE FOR DESIGNING A WALL CARVING

NOTE:
DO NOT INCLUDE IN YOUR SKETCHES
SHARP INTERNAL CORNERS
THESE ARE VERY DIFFICULT TO WORK

ALSO DO NOT INCLUDE THIN LEGS ETC.
ON THE SHORT GRAIN AS THE WOOD
WILL BREAK EASILY

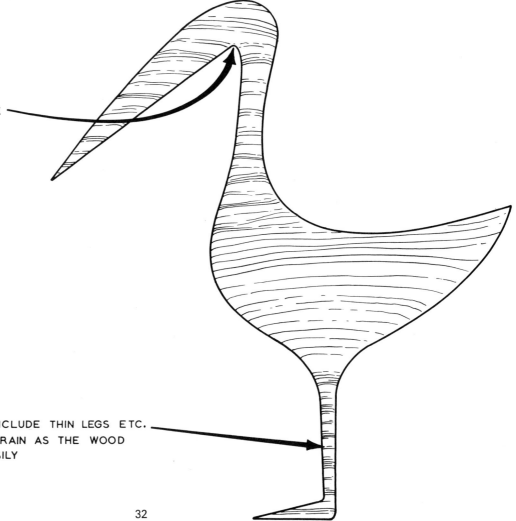

A GUIDE FOR DESIGNING A WALL CARVING

❷

CONSIDER YOUR VARIOUS SKETCHES
THEN CUT OUT THE ONE YOU LIKE BEST

❸

FROM A SUITABLE LENGTH OF MACHINE
FACE PLANED AND THICKNESSED NATURAL
BOARDING PREPARE A PIECE OF TIMBER
TO THE OVERALL MARKING OUT SIZES BELOW

LENGTH OF YOUR PATTERN + 1" (25 mm)

5/8" or 3/4" (16 mm OR 18mm)

PATTERN

WIDTH OF YOUR PATTERN + 1"
(25 mm)

A GUIDE FOR DESIGNING A WALL CARVING

4

DECIDE WHERE YOUR WORK HAS TO BE
TAPERED IN BULK THEN MARK OUT AND
REMOVE THE TAPERS' WASTE WITH A JACK PLANE

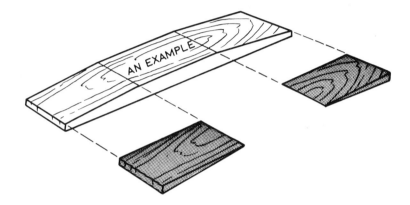

5

TAPE YOUR CUT OUT PATTERN ON THE
BACK OF YOUR TIMBER THEN PENCIL
ALL ROUND THE OUTLINE

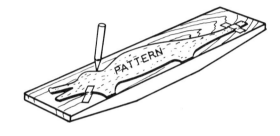

6

REMOVE THE PATTERN THEN
COLOUR IN THE WASTE

7

SHAPE   YOUR

WALL

CARVING

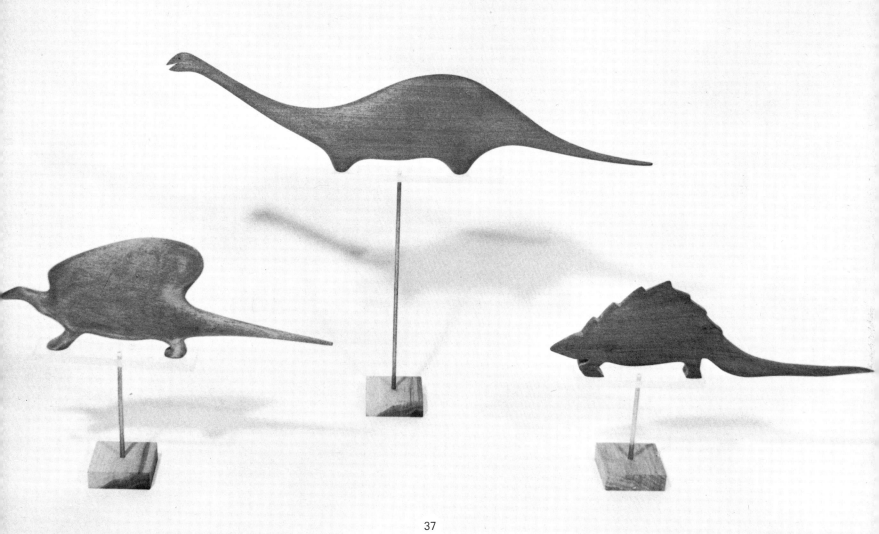

INTRODUCTION TO STANDING CARVINGS

❶

A STANDING CARVING CAN BE
AN ATTRACTIVE ITEM FOR YOUR HOME

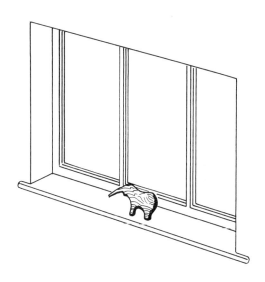

❷

TO PREVENT THE CARVING FROM BEING TOP HEAVY
TAPER THE TIMBER FROM THE BASE UPWARDS

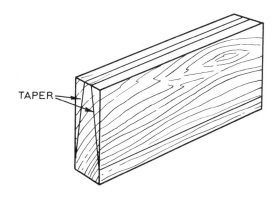

TAPER

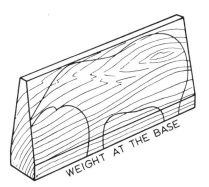

WEIGHT AT THE BASE

INTRODUCTION TO STANDING CARVINGS

3

USE AN ATTRACTIVE CLEAN CUTTING HARDWOOD FOR EASY WORKING

E X A M P L E S

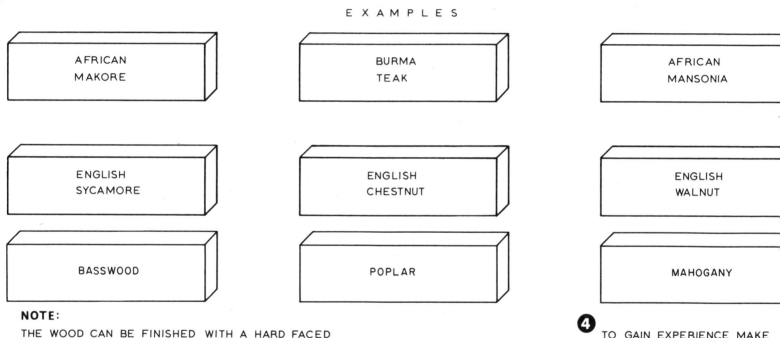

AFRICAN MAKORE

BURMA TEAK

AFRICAN MANSONIA

ENGLISH SYCAMORE

ENGLISH CHESTNUT

ENGLISH WALNUT

BASSWOOD

POPLAR

MAHOGANY

NOTE:

THE WOOD CAN BE FINISHED WITH A HARD FACED
LACQUER OR OIL— OR IT CAN BE LEFT IN ITS NATURAL STATE
CHOOSE THE FINISH TO SUIT THE TYPE OF TIMBER

4

TO GAIN EXPERIENCE MAKE
ONE OR BOTH OF THE SET PIECES
BY FOLLOWING THE WORKING GUIDE

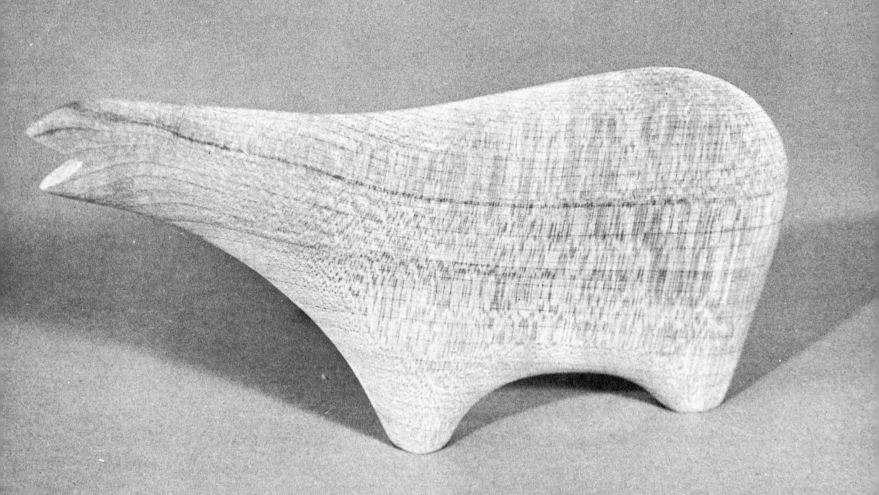

WORKING GUIDE FOR STANDING CARVING SET PIECE Nº1

❶

MAKE A TRACING OF THE FULL SIZE OUTLINE BELOW

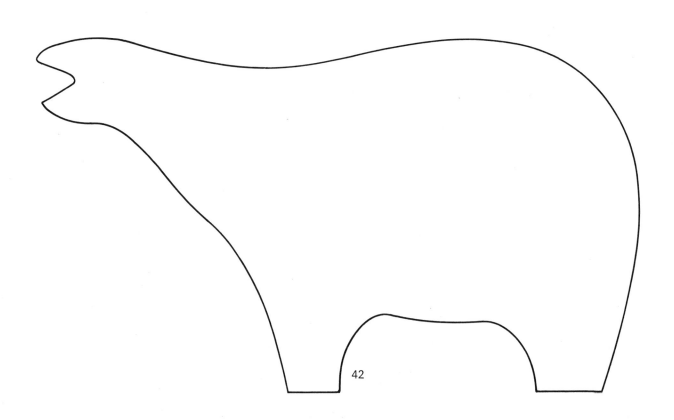

42

WORKING GUIDE FOR STANDING CARVING SET PIECE Nº1

❷

FROM A SUITABLE LENGTH OF MACHINE FACE PLANED
AND THICKNESSED NATURAL BOARDING PREPARE A PIECE
OF TIMBER TO THE OVERALL MARKING
OUT SIZES BELOW

7/8″ (22 mm)

4 1/2″
(115 mm)

8″
(203 mm)

❸

MARK OUT THE TAPERS

1″ (25 mm)

1/4″ (6 mm)

❺

REMOVE THE WASTE
WITH A JACK PLANE
(LEAVE THE LINES JUST IN)

43

❹

COLOUR IN THE WASTE

WORKING GUIDE FOR STANDING CARVING SET PIECE Nº1

6

PIN YOUR TRACING ON THE TAPERED TIMBER
AND TRACE OVER WITH A 3H PENCIL

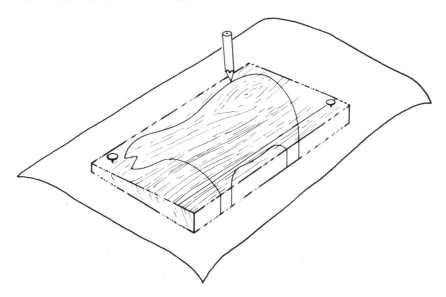

7

REMOVE THE TRACING PAPER AND
PENCIL IN THE IMPRINT

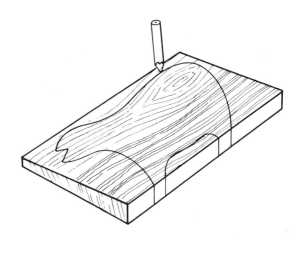

8

SQUARE OVER THE FEET BOTTOMS

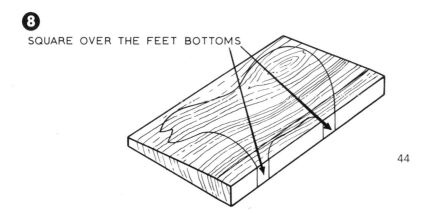

9

COLOUR IN
THE WASTE

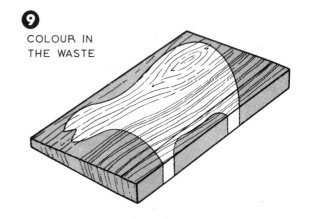

WORKING GUIDE FOR STANDING CARVING SET PIECE №1

10

AT A SUITABLE POSITION MARK OVER A
SQUARE SAWING GUIDE LINE

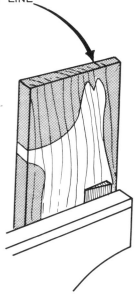

11

REMOVE THE WASTE
WITH A COPING SAW
(LEAVE THE LINES WELL IN)

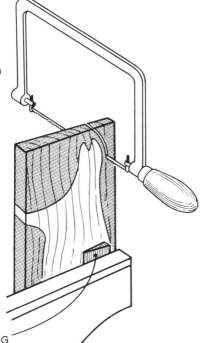

WEDGE PACKING

12

REMOVE ANY LARGE LUMPS
WITH A MEDIUM CUTTING WOOD
RASP THEN CLEAN DOWN TO THE
LINES WITH FINE CUTTING WOOD FILES

CUT WITH
FORWARD STROKE ONLY

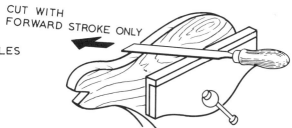

(LEAVE THE LINES JUST IN)

WORKING GUIDE FOR STANDING CARVING SET PIECE № 1

13 REDUCE ANY OUTSTANDING
BULK AND ROUND OFF ANY
SHARP CORNERS WITH
A SUITABLE SPOKESHAVE
AND FINE CUTTING WOOD FILES

14 MARK THE POSITION OF
THE EYES AND BORE
CAREFULLY WITH A BRADAWL

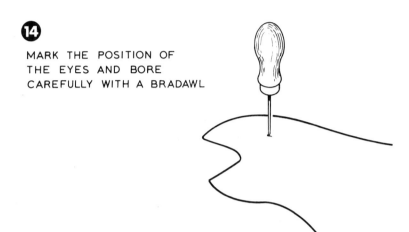

15 CLEAN UP WITH GLASS PAPER
GRADE № M2 THEN GRADE № 1
OR SANDPAPER GRADE № 80 THEN
GRADE № 120

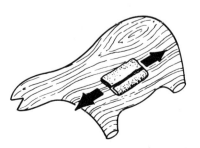

16 APPLY

A

FINISH

?

WORKING GUIDE FOR STANDING CARVING SET PIECE Nº2

1

MAKE A TRACING OF THE
FULL SIZE OUTLINE BELOW

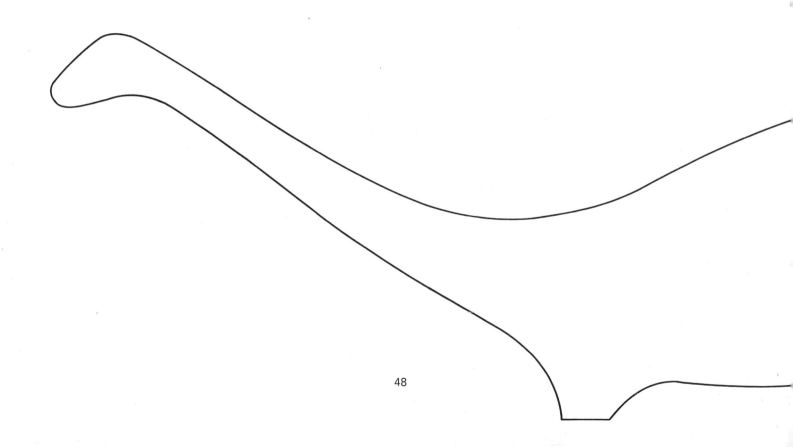

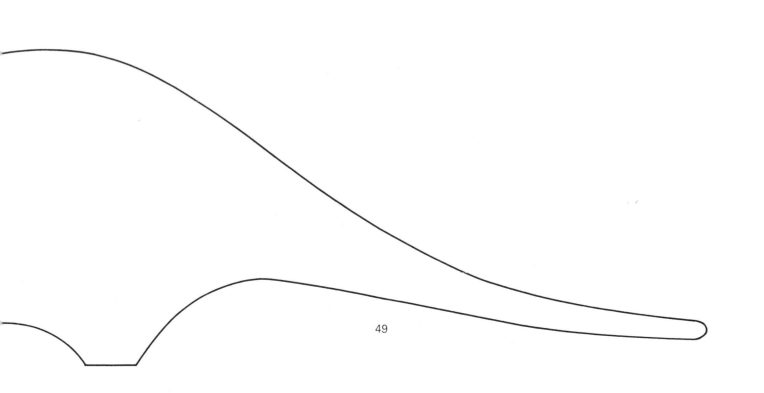

49

WORKING GUIDE FOR STANDING CARVING SET PIECE №2

2

FROM A SUITABLE LENGTH OF MACHINE FACE PLANED
AND THICKNESSED NATURAL BOARDING PREPARE A PIECE
OF TIMBER TO THE OVERALL MARKING OUT SIZES BELOW

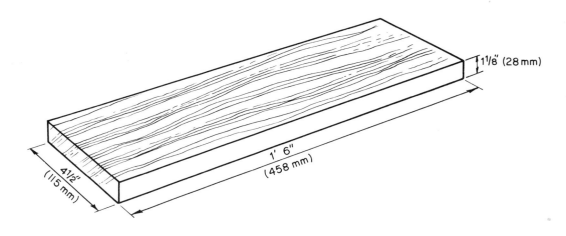

1 1/8" (28 mm)

1' 6"
(458 mm)

4 1/2"
(115 mm)

3

MARK OUT THE TAPERS

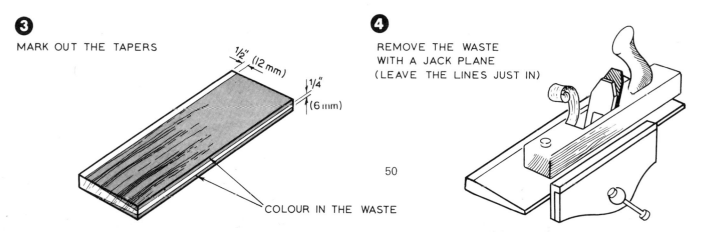

1/2" (12 mm)

1/4"
(6 mm)

COLOUR IN THE WASTE

4

REMOVE THE WASTE
WITH A JACK PLANE
(LEAVE THE LINES JUST IN)

50

WORKING GUIDE FOR STANDING CARVING SET PIECE Nº2

5

PIN YOUR TRACING ON THE TAPERED TIMBER
AND TRACE OVER WITH A 3H PENCIL

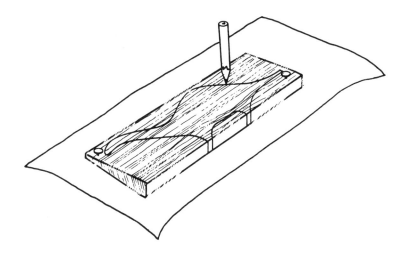

6

REMOVE THE TRACING PAPER AND
PENCIL IN THE IMPRINT

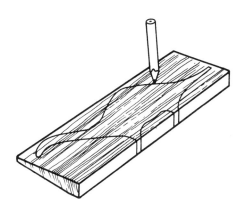

7

SQUARE OVER THE FEET BOTTOMS

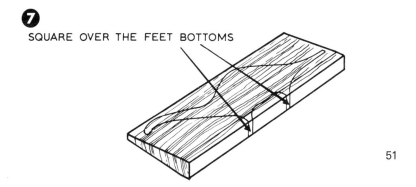

8

COLOUR IN
THE WASTE

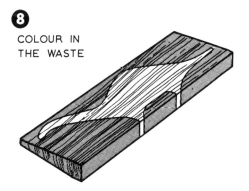

WORKING GUIDE FOR STANDING CARVING SET PIECE Nº2

9

AT A SUITABLE POSITION MARK OVER
A SQUARE SAWING GUIDE LINE

10

REMOVE THE WASTE
WITH A COPING SAW
(LEAVE THE LINES JUST IN)

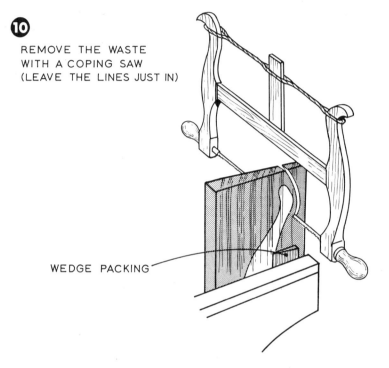

WEDGE PACKING

11

REMOVE ANY LARGE LUMPS WITH A MEDIUM CUTTING
WOOD RASP THEN CLEAN DOWN TO THE LINES
WITH A FINE CUTTING WOOD FILE
(LEAVE THE LINES JUST IN)

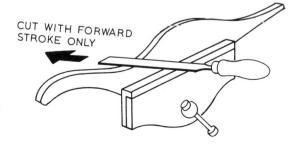

CUT WITH FORWARD
STROKE ONLY

WORKING GUIDE FOR STANDING CARVING SET PIECE №2

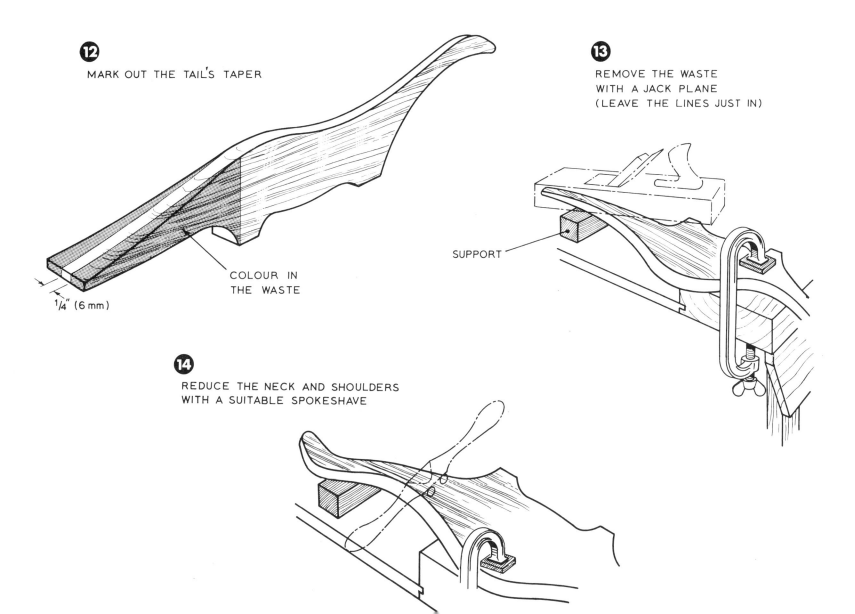

12 MARK OUT THE TAIL'S TAPER

COLOUR IN THE WASTE

1/4" (6 mm)

13 REMOVE THE WASTE WITH A JACK PLANE (LEAVE THE LINES JUST IN)

SUPPORT

14 REDUCE THE NECK AND SHOULDERS WITH A SUITABLE SPOKESHAVE

WORKING GUIDE FOR STANDING CARVING SET PIECE Nº2

14

REDUCE ANY OUTSTANDING BULK AND ROUND OFF ANY
SHARP CORNERS WITH A SUITABLE SPOKESHAVE AND
FINE CUTTING WOOD FILES

15

CLEAN UP WITH GLASS PAPER
GRADE NºM2 THEN GRADE Nº1
OR SANDPAPER GRADE Nº 80 THEN
GRADE Nº120

16

APPLY

A

FINISH

?

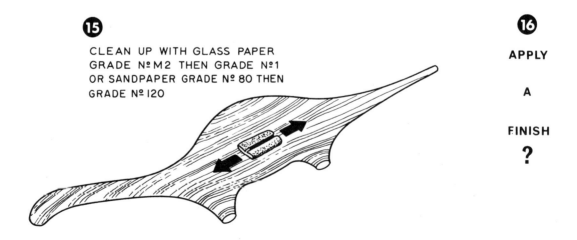

A GUIDE FOR DESIGNING A STANDING CARVING

❶

FIRST DO A NUMBER OF REASONABLY
SIZED SKETCHES ON THICK PAPER
OF SUITABLE THINGS TO CARVE

❷

<u>**REMEMBER**</u>

DO NOT INCLUDE IN YOUR SKETCHES
SHARP INTERNAL CORNERS AS THEY
ARE VERY DIFFICULT TO WORK

ALSO DO NOT INCLUDE THIN LEGS ETC
ON THE SHORT GRAIN AS THE WOOD
MAY BREAK EASILY

❸

IDEAS FOR SKETCHES CAN BE OBTAINED

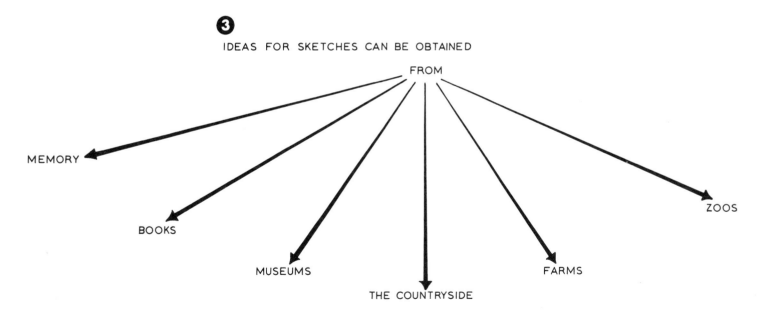

FROM

MEMORY

BOOKS

MUSEUMS

THE COUNTRYSIDE

FARMS

ZOOS

A GUIDE FOR DESIGNING A STANDING CARVING

4

CONSIDER YOUR VARIOUS SKETCHES
THEN CUT OUT THE ONE YOU LIKE BEST

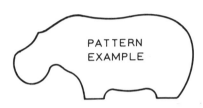

PATTERN
EXAMPLE

5

FROM A SUITABLE LENGTH OF MACHINE
FACE PLANED AND THICKNESSED NATURAL
BOARDING PREPARE A PIECE OF TIMBER
TO THE OVERALL MARKING OUT SIZES BELOW

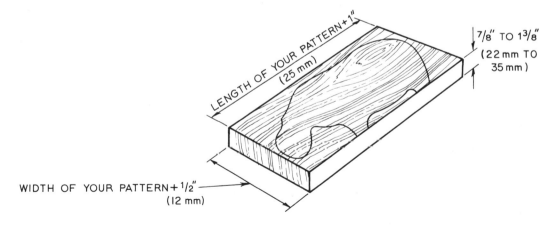

LENGTH OF YOUR PATTERN + 1"
(25 mm)

7/8" TO 1 3/8"
(22 mm TO
35 mm)

WIDTH OF YOUR PATTERN + 1/2"
(12 mm)

A GUIDE FOR DESIGNING A STANDING CARVING

6

ON THE PREPARED TIMBER
MARK OUT A SUITABLE TAPER
(GUIDE BELOW)

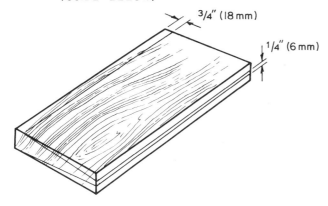

3/4" (18 mm)

1/4" (6 mm)

7

COLOUR IN
THE WASTE

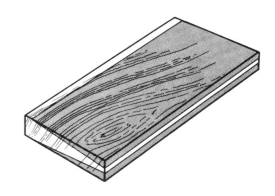

8

REMOVE THE WASTE WITH A JACK PLANE
(LEAVE THE LINES JUST IN)

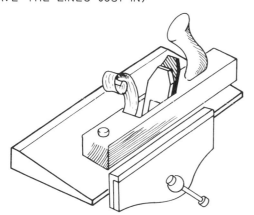

9

TAPE YOUR CUT OUT PATTERN
ON A TAPERED FACE
THEN PENCIL ALL ROUND THE OUTLINE

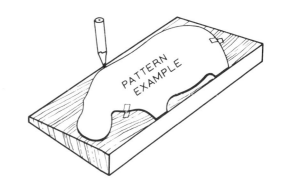

PATTERN EXAMPLE

A GUIDE FOR DESIGNING A STANDING CARVING

10 REMOVE THE PATTERN

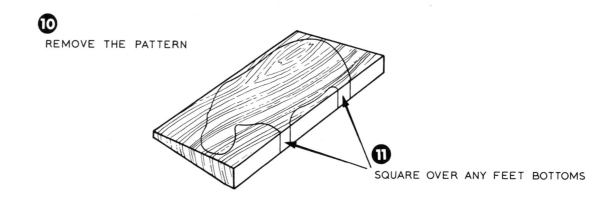

11 SQUARE OVER ANY FEET BOTTOMS

12 COLOUR IN THE WASTE

13 SHAPE YOUR

STANDING

CARVING

60

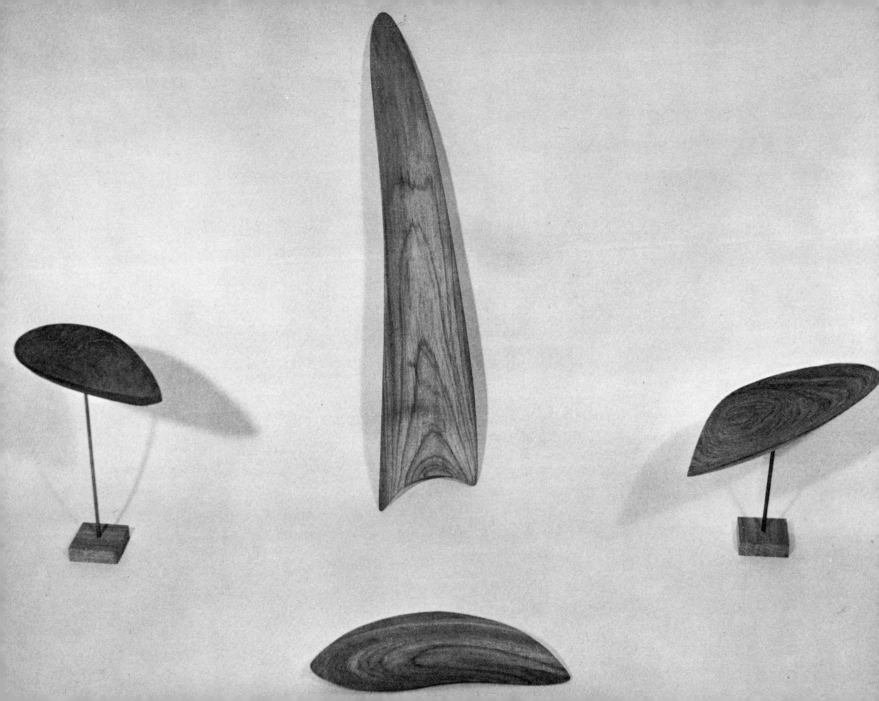

INTRODUCTION TO BOWL CARVINGS

❶

SHALLOW WOOD BOWLS HAVE MANY USES
IN THE HOME. FOR EXAMPLE THEY CAN BE
USED AS FRUIT BOWLS OR AS DISHES
TO HOLD TRINKETS ETC

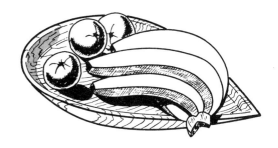

❷

IT IS ADVISABLE TO BEVEL THE
OUTER EDGE SO THAT THE BOWL
CAN EASILY BE GRIPPED FOR

OR

AN ALTERNATIVE IS TO SHAPE A LARGE
BEVEL AT ONE CORNER TO FORM
A TAIL-LIKE HANDLE

— LIFTING —

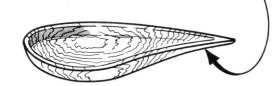

INTRODUCTION TO BOWL CARVINGS

USE A CLEAN CUTTING GOOD QUALITY TIMBER

E X A M P L E S

BURMA TEAK

HONDURAS MAHOGANY

AFRICAN LIMBA
(IF FIRST CLASS A CHEAPER ALTERNATIVE)

ENGLISH CHESTNUT
(IF FIRST CLASS A CHEAPER ALTERNATIVE)

BASSWOOD

❹

NOTE:

THE FINISH CAN BE A HARD FACED LACQUER, OR OIL,
OR THE WOOD CAN BE LEFT WITH A NATURAL FINISH
CHOOSE YOUR FINISH TO SUIT THE TYPE OF TIMBER

INTRODUCTION TO BOWL CARVINGS

❺

ONE METHOD OF HOLDING YOUR WORK
FOR HOLLOWING OUT IS WITH **'G'** CRAMPS

(EXAMPLE)

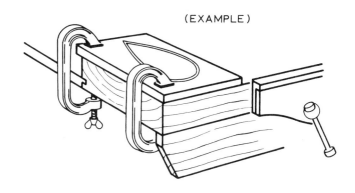

❻

NOTE:
WHEN HOLLOWING OUT A LONG BOWL
PLACE A BOARD UNDERNEATH FOR A
SUPPORT OVER THE WELL OF THE BENCH

BOARD SUPPORT

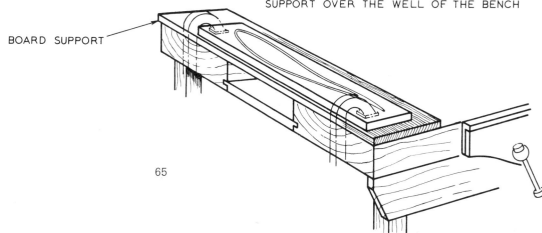

INTRODUCTION TO BOWL CARVINGS

7 SUITABLE GOUGES FOR HOLLOWING OUT THE CENTRE

THE STRAIGHT GOUGE № 4

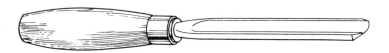

¾" (18mm)

SUITABLE SWEEP

USED FOR REMOVING THE BULK
OF THE WASTE AND LEVELLING
THE BOTTOM OF THE BOWL

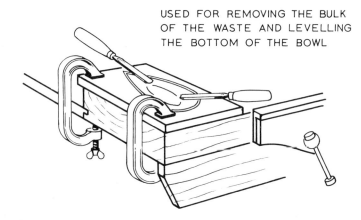

THE STRAIGHT GOUGE № 6

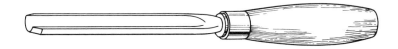

¾" (18mm)

SUITABLE SWEEP

USED FOR REMOVING THE WASTE
NEAR THE INNER RIM LINE

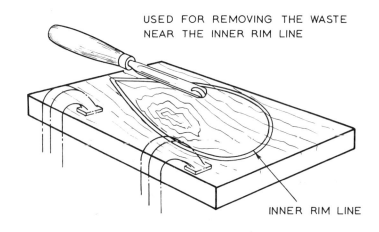

INNER RIM LINE

INTRODUCTION TO BOWL CARVINGS

8

SUITABLE GOUGES FOR HOLLOWING OUT THE CENTRE

THE OUT-CHANNEL FIRMER GOUGE

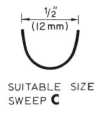

SUITABLE SIZE
SWEEP **C**

USED FOR CLEANING OUT NARROW CORNERS
AND FLUTED FINISHING

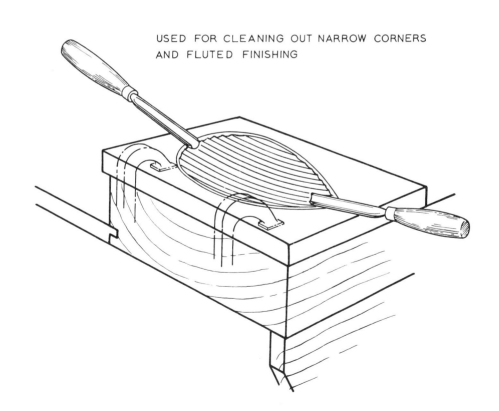

INTRODUCTION TO BOWL CARVINGS

9 REMEMBER TO REMOVE THE WASTE CAREFULLY
AND CHECK THE DEPTH OF YOUR WORK OFTEN

DEPTH CHECK

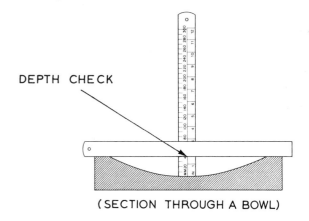

(SECTION THROUGH A BOWL)

10 IF YOU DO NOT
THIS MAY WELL HAPPEN **!**

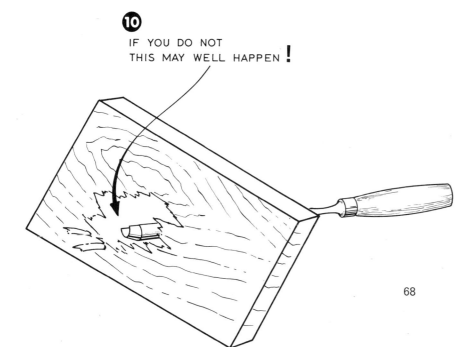

11 TO GAIN EXPERIENCE MAKE
THE PRACTICE BOWL BY
FOLLOWING THE WORKING GUIDE

WORKING GUIDE FOR PRACTICE BOWL

1

MAKE A TRACING OF THE FULL SIZE
INNER RIM AND OUTLINE BELOW

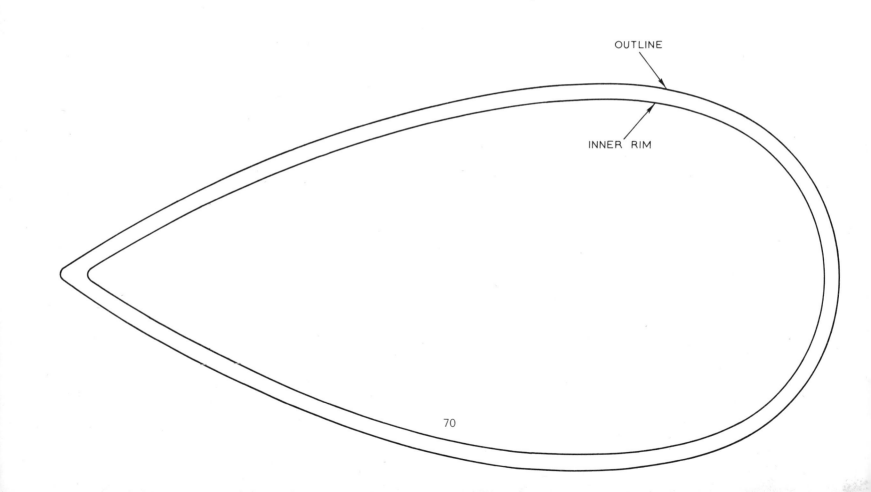

OUTLINE

INNER RIM

70

WORKING GUIDE FOR PRACTICE BOWL

❷

FROM A SUITABLE LENGTH OF MACHINE FACE PLANED
AND THICKNESSED NATURAL BOARDING PREPARE A PIECE
OF TIMBER TO THE OVERALL MARKING OUT SIZES BELOW

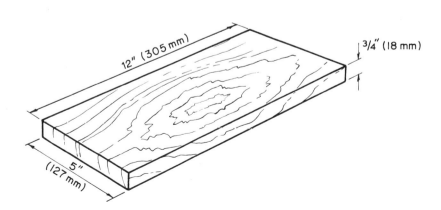

WORKING GUIDE FOR PRACTICE BOWL

❸

PIN YOUR TRACING ON THE TIMBER
AND TRACE OVER WITH A 3H PENCIL

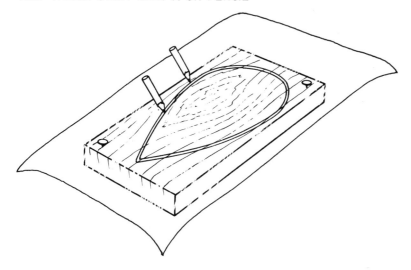

❹

REMOVE THE TRACING PAPER
AND PENCIL IN THE PENCIL IMPRINTS

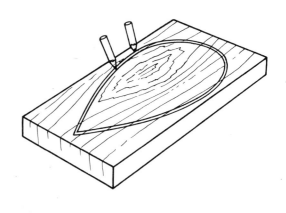

❺

COLOUR IN
THE INNER WASTE

❻

FASTEN YOUR

WORK DOWN

FOR HOLLOWING

72

WORKING GUIDE FOR PRACTICE BOWL

7

FOR A SMOOTH FINISH

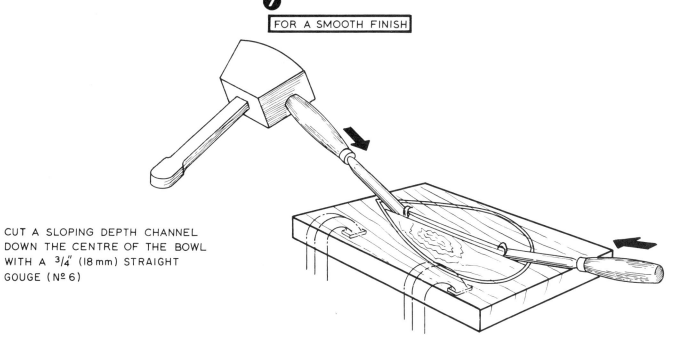

CUT A SLOPING DEPTH CHANNEL
DOWN THE CENTRE OF THE BOWL
WITH A $3/4''$ (18 mm) STRAIGHT
GOUGE (N° 6)

LEAVE AT LEAST $1/4''$ (6 mm) AT THE CENTRE AND WORK IN DIRECTION OF ARROWS

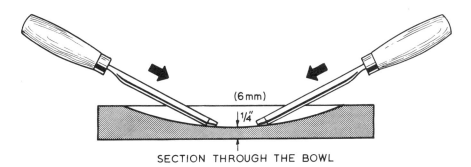

(6 mm)

$1/4''$

SECTION THROUGH THE BOWL

WORKING GUIDE FOR PRACTICE BOWL

 8

FOR A SMOOTH FINISH

REMOVE THE BULK OF THE
WASTE AT THE CENTRE
WITH A $\frac{3}{4}''$ (18 mm) STRAIGHT
GOUGE (Nº 4)

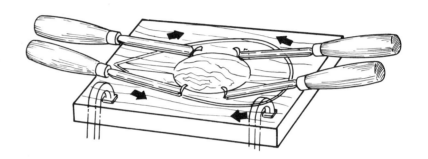

REMOVE THE BULK OF THE WASTE NEAR THE
INNER RIM LINE WITH A $\frac{3}{4}''$ (18 mm) STRAIGHT GOUGE (Nº 6) LEAVE THE LINES JUST IN

USE AN OUT-CHANNELLED GOUGE
FOR WORKING AT THE POINT

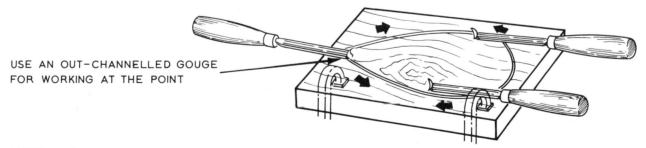

NOTE:
WORK IN THE DIRECTION OF THE ARROWS AND STOP WHEN THE GRAIN STARTS TO CUT UP THEN WORK
THE OTHER WAY

WORKING GUIDE FOR PRACTICE BOWL

FOR A SMOOTH FINISH

LEVEL THOROUGHLY WITH A STRAIGHT GOUGE ($^3/_4$" (18 mm) SWEEP Nº 5)

WORK IN THE DIRECTION OF THE ARROWS
AND STOP WHEN THE GRAIN STARTS TO
CUT UP THEN WORK THE OTHER WAY

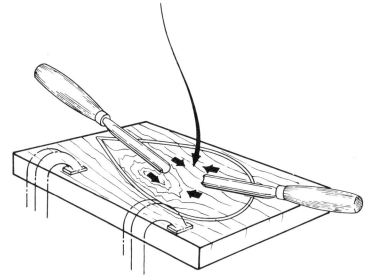

THOROUGHLY CLEAN UP THE HOLLOWED OUT CENTRE WITH GLASS PAPER GRADE Nº M2
OR SANDPAPER GRADE Nº 80

WORKING GUIDE FOR PRACTICE BOWL

FLUTED FINISH DETAILS ONLY

FIRST REMOVE THE BULK AT THE CENTRE TO A DEPTH OF $\frac{1}{2}$" (12 mm) THEN WORK BACK TO THE INNER RIM LINE WITH AN OUT CHANNELLED FIRMER GOUGE ($\frac{1}{2}$" (12 mm) SWEEP C)

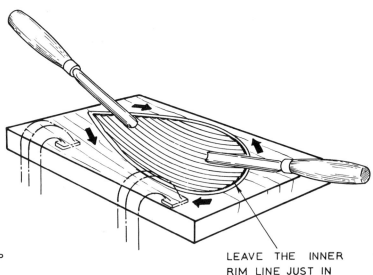

NOTE:
WORK IN THE DIRECTION OF THE ARROWS AND STOP WHEN THE GRAIN STARTS TO CUT UP THEN WORK THE OTHER WAY

LEAVE THE INNER RIM LINE JUST IN

WORKING GUIDE FOR PRACTICE BOWL

11 RELEASE THE BOWL

12 COLOUR IN
THE OUTSIDE WASTE

13 AT A SUITABLE POSITION
MARK OVER A SQUARE
SAWING GUIDE LINE

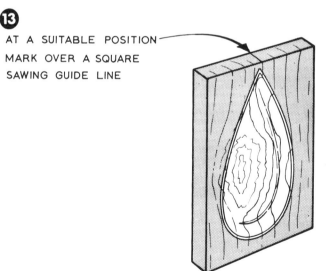

WORKING GUIDE FOR PRACTICE BOWL

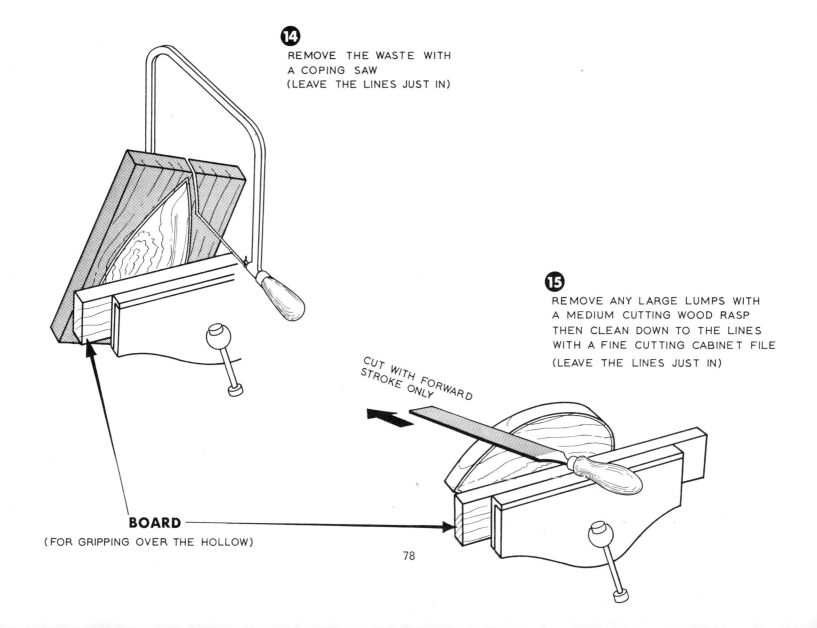

14

REMOVE THE WASTE WITH
A COPING SAW
(LEAVE THE LINES JUST IN)

15

REMOVE ANY LARGE LUMPS WITH
A MEDIUM CUTTING WOOD RASP
THEN CLEAN DOWN TO THE LINES
WITH A FINE CUTTING CABINET FILE
(LEAVE THE LINES JUST IN)

CUT WITH FORWARD
STROKE ONLY

BOARD
(FOR GRIPPING OVER THE HOLLOW)

78

WORKING GUIDE FOR PRACTICE BOWL

16 MARK OUT THE EDGE BEVEL

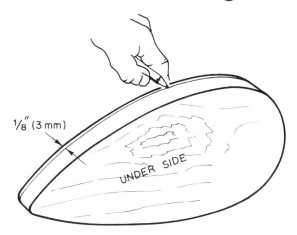

1/8" (3 mm)

UNDER SIDE

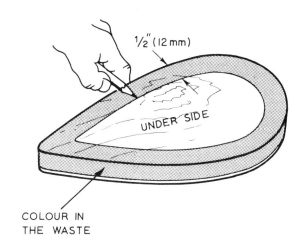

1/2" (12 mm)

UNDER SIDE

COLOUR IN
THE WASTE

17 REMOVE THE WASTE WITH
A SUITABLE SPOKESHAVE
(LEAVE THE LINES JUST IN)

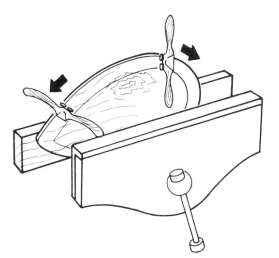

18

CLEAN ALL ROUND WITH GLASS
PAPER GRADE № M2 THEN GRADE № 1
OR SANDPAPER GRADE № 80 THEN
GRADE № 120

19

APPLY

A

FINISH

?

A GUIDE FOR DESIGNING A CARVED BOWL

 1

FIRST ASSEMBLE THE THINGS
WHICH WILL BE PLACED IN YOUR BOWL

(EXAMPLE)

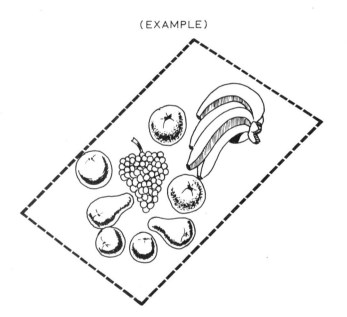

 2

THEN NOTE THE OVERALL AREA

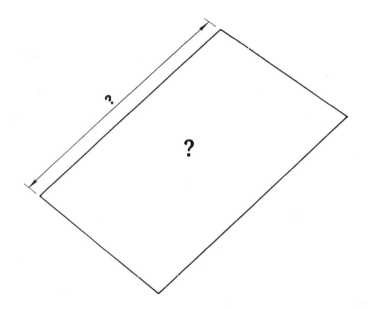

A GUIDE FOR DESIGNING A CARVED BOWL

❸

ON A LARGE SHEET OF DRAWING PAPER
SCRIBE CONTINUOUS LOOPS
IN FIGURE EIGHT PATTERNS

NOTE:
MAKE THE AREA OF EACH LOOP
ROUGHLY EQUAL TO THE AREA
YOU HAVE DECIDED ON

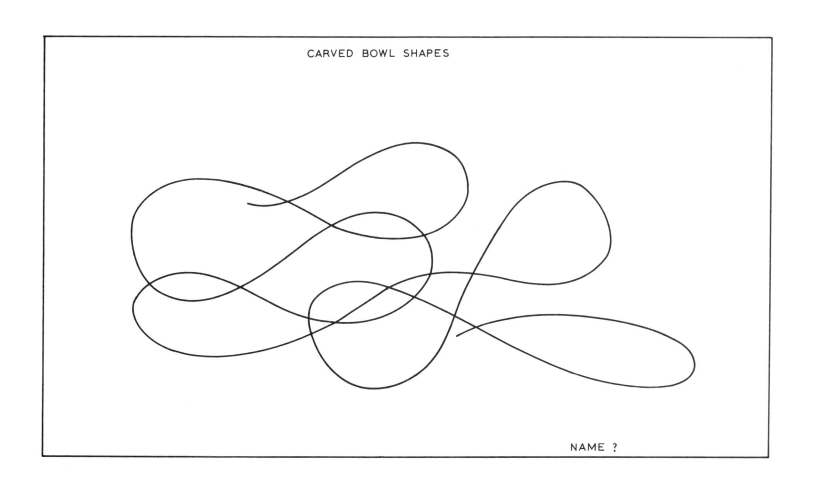

CARVED BOWL SHAPES

NAME ?

A GUIDE FOR DESIGNING A CARVED BOWL

4 LOOK AT THE VARIOUS SHAPES FORMED
ON YOUR PAPER AND LINE IN THE MOST
PLEASING ONES
      (EXAMPLES BELOW)

5 NOW CHOOSE THE ONE YOU LIKE
THE BEST THEN CUT IT OUT

PATTERN EXAMPLE

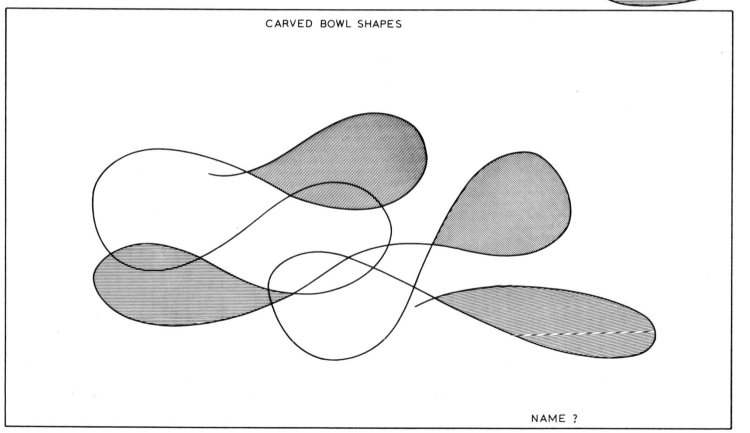

CARVED BOWL SHAPES

NAME ?

A GUIDE FOR DESIGNING A CARVED BOWL

6

FROM A SUITABLE LENGTH OF MACHINE FACE PLANED
AND THICKNESSED NATURAL BOARDING PREPARE A PIECE
OF TIMBER TO THE OVERALL MARKING OUT SIZES BELOW

LENGTH OF YOUR PATTERN+3" (75 mm)

PATTERN EXAMPLE

$^3/_4$" TO $1^3/_8$"
(18 mm TO 35 mm)

WIDTH OF YOUR PATTERN + 1"
(25 mm)

7

TAPE YOUR CUT OUT PATTERN ON THE TIMBER
THEN PENCIL ALL ROUND THE OUTLINE

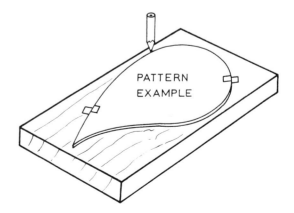

PATTERN EXAMPLE

A GUIDE FOR DESIGNING A CARVED BOWL

8

REMOVE YOUR PATTERN

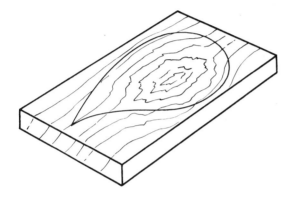

9

SKETCH IN THE
INNER RIM LINE

$3/16''$ (5 mm)

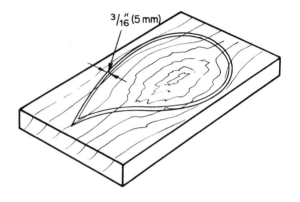

10

COLOUR IN
THE INNER WASTE

11

HOLLOW OUT

AND SHAPE

YOUR BOWL

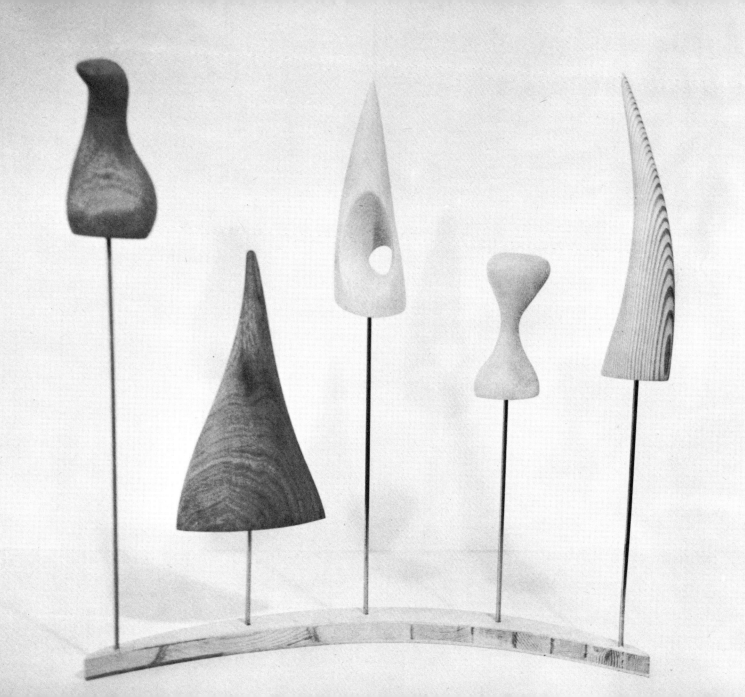

INTRODUCTION TO ABSTRACT WOOD SCULPTURE

❶

ABSTRACT WOOD SCULPTURE CAN BE AN
ATTRACTIVE ORNAMENT FOR YOUR HOME

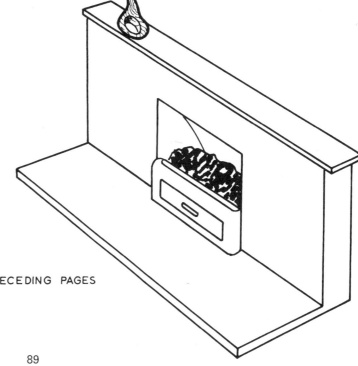

❷

HAVE A CLOSE LOOK AT THE PHOTOGRAPHS
OF ABSTRACT WOOD SCULPTURE ON THE THREE PRECEDING PAGES

INTRODUCTION TO ABSTRACT WOOD SCULPTURE

3

TRY TO AVOID FORMING
SHARP CORNERS

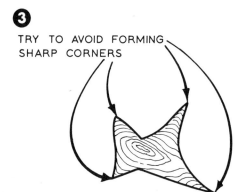

A COMBINATION OF SUPPLE CURVES
OFTEN LOOKS MUCH BETTER AND
IS EASIER TO WORK

4

IF YOU WANT YOUR WORK
TO STAND UPRIGHT LEAVE
ONE END FLAT AS A BASE

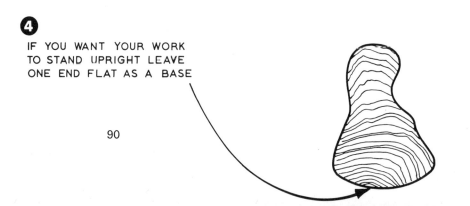

INTRODUCTION TO ABSTRACT WOOD SCULPTURE

❺

IT IS NOT EASY TO GRIP IRREGULAR SHAPES FIRMLY WHILE
THEY ARE BEING WORKED. MUCH THOUGHT AND CARE MUST BE TAKEN

EXAMPLES

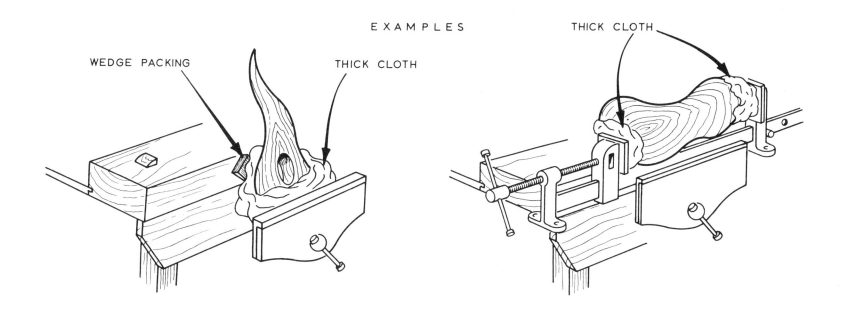

WEDGE PACKING

THICK CLOTH

THICK CLOTH

❻

NOW FOLLOW THE GUIDE FOR DESIGNING AND MAKING AN ABSTRACT WOOD SCULPTURE

A GUIDE FOR DESIGNING AND MAKING AN ABSTRACT WOOD SCULPTURE

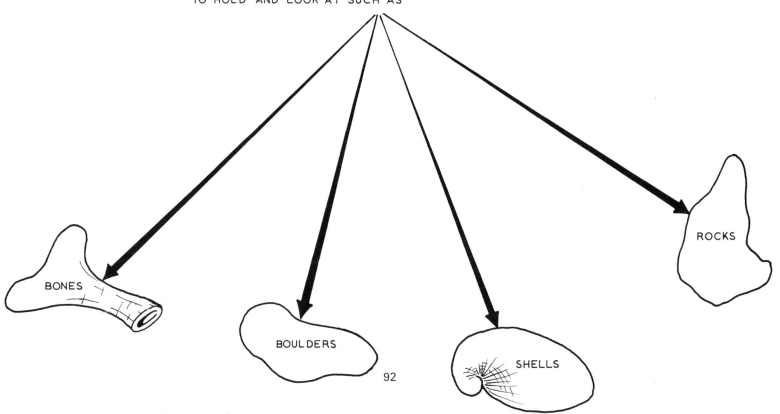

❶
WHENEVER YOU CAN, OBTAIN PERMISSION TO VISIT RUBBISH DUMPS,
HEDGE ROWS, BUILDING SITES, BUILDERS YARDS, BEACHES
BUTCHERS YARDS AND SLAUGHTER HOUSES ETC. FIND AND BRING
TO SCHOOL OBJECTS WHICH ARE INTERESTING AND PLEASANT
TO HOLD AND LOOK AT SUCH AS

BONES

BOULDERS

SHELLS

ROCKS

A GUIDE FOR DESIGNING AND MAKING AN ABSTRACT WOOD SCULPTURE

②

THOROUGHLY INVESTIGATE WITH
YOUR HANDS AND YOUR EYES ALL
THE OBJECTS BROUGHT INTO THE
WORKSHOP

③

THEN, WITH SOME CLAY ON AN OLD BOARD
EXPERIMENT IN FORMING PLEASANT
SHAPES OF YOUR OWN

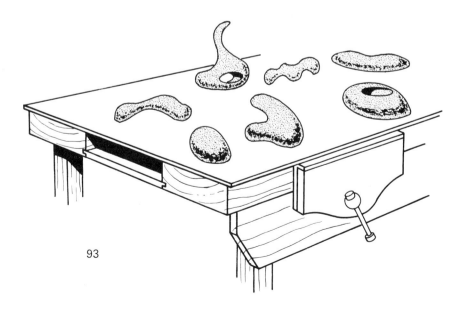

93

A GUIDE FOR DESIGNING AND MAKING AN ABSTRACT WOOD SCULPTURE

4 FIND OR SAW OFF A NOG OF TIMBER OF A SUITABLE SIZE AND VARIETY

EXAMPLES OF SUITABLE SIZES

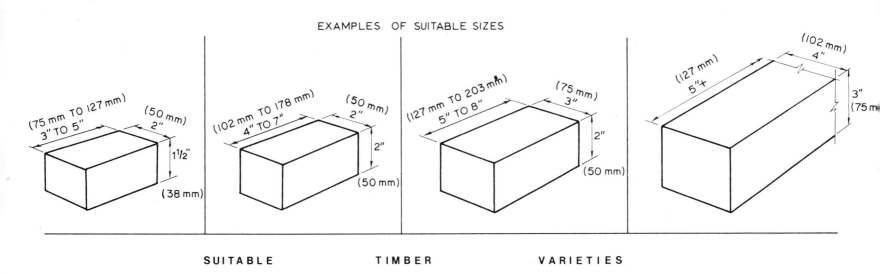

SUITABLE   TIMBER   VARIETIES

ENGLISH SYCAMORE   BURMA TEAK   ENGLISH CHESTNUT

BASSWOOD   INDIAN ROSEWOOD   ENGLISH LABURNUM   MAHOGANY

AFRICAN MANSONIA   AMERICAN BLACK WALNUT   AFRICAN MAKORE

A GUIDE FOR DESIGNING AND MAKING AN ABSTRACT WOOD SCULPTURE

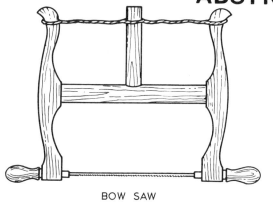

BOW SAW

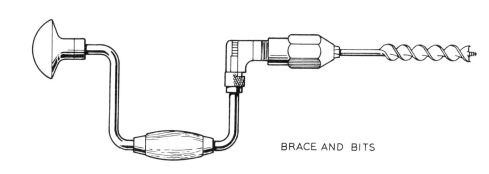

BRACE AND BITS

STRAIGHT GOUGE

CURVED GOUGE

OUT-CHANNELLED FIRMER GOUGE

NOW BEING GUIDED BY TOUCH
SIGHT AND THE FLOW OF THE
GRAIN, USE THESE TOOLS
TO FORM A SHAPE OF YOUR OWN

SPOKESHAVE

(ROUND AND FLAT FACED)

JACK PLANE

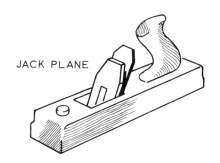

MEDIUM CUTTING WOOD RASP

FINE RAT-TAIL WOOD FILE

FINE CABINET FILE

A GUIDE FOR DESIGNING AND MAKING AN ABSTRACT WOOD SCULPTURE

 6

IF A SMOOTH FINISH IS REQUIRED CLEAN UP FINALLY
WITH FINE-CUTTING WOOD FILES AND GLASS PAPER

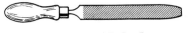

FINE CABINET FILE

FINE RAT-TAIL FILE

GLASS PAPER GRADE M2	THEN	GLASS PAPER GRADE Nº 1
OR		OR
SANDPAPER GRADE Nº 80	THEN	SANDPAPER GRADE Nº 120

IT OFTEN PROVES DIFFICULT TO APPLY
A FINISH TO THIS KIND OF WOOD SCULPTURE
BUT IT GENERALLY LOOKS BETTER
WITHOUT ONE ANYWAY